Sumary

Bachelor Nation
Amy Kaufman

Conversation Starters

By BookHabits

Please Note: This is an unofficial Conversation Starters guide. If you have not yet read the original work, you can purchase the original book here.

We hope you enjoy this complementary guide from BookHabits. Our mission is to aid readers and reading groups with quality, thought provoking material to in the discovery and discussions on some of today's favorite books.

Bonus Downloads
*Get Free Books with **<u>Any Purchase</u>** of* Conversation Starters!

Every purchase comes with a FREE download!

Add spice to any conversation
Never run out of things to say
Spend time with those you love

Get it Now

or Click Here.

Scan Your Phone

Tips for Using Conversation Starters:

EVERY GOOD BOOK CONTAINS A WORLD FAR DEEPER THAN the surface of its pages. Questions herein are designed to bring us beneath the surface of the page and invite us into the world that lives on. These questions can be used to:

- Foster a deeper understanding of the book
- Promote an atmosphere of discussion for groups
- Assist in the study of the book, either individually or corporately
- Explore unseen realms of the book as never seen before

Table of Contents

Introducing *Bachelor Nation* 6

Discussion Questions 13

Introducing the Author 34

Fireside Questions... 40

Quiz Questions 51

Quiz Answers... 64

Ways to Continue Your Reading 65

Introducing *Bachelor Nation*

*B*ACHELOR NATION: INSIDE THE WORLD OF AMERICA'S FAVORITE GUILTY PLEASURE hit the shelves and would quickly be snatched off them before the book could gather a speck of dust. Amy Kaufman, writer at the *Los Angeles Times* and author of her debut *Bachelor Nation*, went behind the scenes of the famous TV reality show to give readers an exclusive look that stays hidden behind the cameras which in the end got her blacklisted from ABC events.

Every human is fascinated with schadenfreude. People can't help looking when there is trouble in the air whether it is a fire or a car accident. Humans also find a good love story heartwarming and soul-smiling. The reality show *The Bachelor* has combined love and schadenfreude into a series that millions are captivated by. Amy Kaufman, a fellow fan of the show, was able to go behind the camera and see what really happens on the show that isn't staged and was more than happy to divulge the details. Kaufman begins her narrative of the backstage details through numerous interviews with past contestants as well as old and current crew members on how the set-environment is created and how the producers do their best to manipulate the beautiful contestants to do and say things they normally wouldn't. Kaufman was able to reveal that the manipulations began with sequestering the contestants within their set, including keeping all cell-phones, internet, television and visits away from the girls. Alcohol was freely provided to help create a warm, loose feeling to make the contestants more relaxed and willing to let go. At all times the girls could only speak of the bachelor in question to create a bubble around them so that their lives for time only revolved around the show. Lastly, the producers would create extreme dates, which scientifically made the contestants feel as if they are falling in love due to the high-stress situations they are placed in during the dates. The producers were able to get all of these locations and travel free for their show by selling themselves as being valuable to have as customers and free advertisement in the show. Something that Kaufman noticed about the show was how there was a certain amount of racism and stereotypes running as an undercurrent through out the silk and champagne. Kaufman found internal documents that stated that contestants gave ABC permission to reveal personal information no matter how shocking, humiliating or derogatory. Kaufman also found notes from the producers about past contestants that helped them choose who to they wanted as a contestant by specifically looking for people that would create drama and tension within the house. One of Kaufman's most shocking detail she revealed was how the early producers would keep track of the contestant's menstrual cycles so they could have more emotional interviews.

The second theme throughout the book is the reason why people love the show *The Bachelor* so much. Kaufman's theory for this is that the show helps people see what the idea of true love can look like. While most people are trying to find a nice man, the reality show has a man that shows chivalry and courtship as he woos these different women. While the extreme, over-the-top dates may be a bit much for some people, these same people may harbor secrets about desiring these types of dates from the men or women they have a crush on. Another thought that Kaufman wrote about in *Bachelor Nation* is that people enjoy judging the mistakes the contestants constantly make during the show. Of course, some of the mistakes and drama are created by the producers and large amounts of alcohol on the set, but that is not shown on the screen, as Kaufman reveals. Of course, Kaufman realizes that there are millions of reasons why someone would love the show. These were just her own ideas on what she thinks may be the reasonings behind those who watch the show every week and makes their own guesses as to who will be given the rose.

Kaufman hopes to show with her book, *Bachelor Nation: Inside the World of America's Favorite Guilty Pleasure* the difference between what is happening on the screen and what is happening in real life that isn't being shown.

However, despite what is shown through her research, she hopes that the show will change to become better. She hopes that the show will change to make it so that there isn't as much of a difference between what is happening on screen and off screen. Kaufman finishes her writing with the promise that in the meantime she will continue to faithfully watch the show every season.

Discussion Questions

"Get Ready to Enter a New World"

Tip: Begin with questions dealing with broader issues to ensure ample time for quality discussions. Read through all discussion questions before engaging.

~~~

question 1

Why do you think people are interested in watching the drama that happens on *The Bachelor*?

~~~

~~~

question 2

After reading *Bachelor Nation*, were you surprised by any of the details that Kaufman goes over?

~~~

~ ~ ~

question 3

Considering the show is about a man falling in love with a woman out of many, do you think that the love is real, especially after Kaufman reveals that the producers create the moments? Why or why not?

~ ~ ~

~~~

question 4

Kaufman wrote that she hopes the show could change so that what happens behind the camera isn't as shocking to learn about. How do you think the show could go about doing that?

~~~

~~~

question 5

Kaufman wrote how she saw the show being racist. Do you agree with that statement? Why or why not?

~~~

~ ~ ~

question 6

Kaufman wrote how the producers isolate the contestants when they arrive at the house. How do you think that makes the contestants feel?

~ ~ ~

~~~

question 7

Kaufman wrote that the contestants can only talk about the bachelor they are trying to win over. How do you think they feel about that rule?

~~~

~~~

question 8

Considering the contestants can only talk about the bachelor, do you think it makes them like him more? Why or why not?

~~~

~~~

question 9

Do you think it would be easy to be a contestant on the show. Why or why not?

~~~

~~~

question 10

The Bachelor is about a man finding his wife. Why do you think people like to watch love stories, even if they may not be completely real?

~~~

~ ~ ~

question 11

Kaufman wrote about how she learned the contestants sign a contract that gives the producers the right to publish anything about the contestant's lives, no matter how damaging. Do you think the contestants knew what that really entailed? How do you think they felt when they signed that contract?

~ ~ ~

~~~

question 12

Kaufman revealed that the producers pick
contestants they know will create tension and rift.
How do you feel after you found that out?

~~~

~~~

question 13

Kaufman revealed that the show is able to get free hotel rooms and event planning from saying their show will make the places more popular. Do you think that is ethical of the show to promise that in return for free product and services?

~~~

~~~

question 14

The producers make the contestants feel like they
are falling in love by putting them in high-stress
situations. Do you think that is ethical? Why or
why not?

~~~

~ ~ ~

question 15

Kaufman wrote that ABC banned her from events after her book was published. Why do you think that was?

~ ~ ~

question 16

One reviewer stated that they felt Kaufman's book showed a truth about American culture. What do you think that truth is?

~~~

~~~

question 17

One reviewer stated that Kaufman's book showed the psyche of the show. Do you agree? What are some examples of that?

~~~

~~~

question 18

One reviewer stated that Kaufman's book will play a role in the future of feminism and gender studies. Do you agree? Why or why not?

~~~

question 19

One reviewer was disgusted about how the producers would track the female contestant's menstrual cycles in order to gain more emotional interviews. Do you agree with the reviewer? Why or why not?

~~~

~~~

question 20

One reviewer was upset that they realized producers used sound bites to create different meanings than what they originally had. Do you agree with this reviewer? Why or why not?

~~~

Introducing the Author

AMY KAUFMAN IS A WRITER FOR THE *LA TIMES* WHERE SHE keeps her eyes and ears open for any stories she could write about that are about pop culture, celebrities and film. She reported about many famous events such as the Academy Awards, Golden Globes and the Sundance Film Festival. Kaufman also pursues and writes profiles on many of the stars that are in the limelight. She has worked with and written about famous stars such as Jane Goodall, Lady Gaga and Carly Simon. Kaufman is most known for getting into the Hollywood drama and pointing out how much the rag magazines lie about the people in the spotlight. When Kaufman learned that James Franco's halo wasn't as shiny as it supposedly was, she was more than happy to let the world know about how he would use his status to make sexual harassment advances to the women who took his acting class and looked up to him. Kaufman also wrote in her articles about the sexual harassment allegations against the famous producer, Brett Ratner. With her skill and tenacity in finding the truth about the spider web known as Hollywood, it made sense for Amy Kaufman to go for one of her favorite shows and find out what makes it tick. Her debut book, *Bachelor Nation: Inside the World of America's Favorite Guilty Pleasure* was an instant *New York Times* Bestseller the minute it landed on the shelves of the bookstore. Within its pages, Kaufman wrote about the good and the bad about the show that she watches religiously herself. Kaufman admitted in an interview that she received inspiration to write her book after watching *UnREAL*. She wanted to know if what was being shown was in fact true, thus leading her to do her own research and writing her book. Unfortunately, Kaufman has received flack from those who work on the big hit show *The Bachelor* after her book was published. After a blog post in 2012 about Ben Flajnik's episode called "Women Tell All" where Kaufman revealed an unaired moment of an interaction between the producer Elan Gale and the winner of Flajnik's season,

Courtney Robertson, where Courtney was positioned to appear as the villain, Kaufman was banned by ABC to their future events. Kaufman found out about the banning when she was denied access to a conference call and a call to her editor asking why she had been denied; ABC told Kaufman's editor that her book's coverage of the show was too negative for them. Since then, she has since had trouble with future engagements such as being called a "moron" by *The Bachelor*'s creator, Mike Fleiss, and having a tour of the new *Bachelor* mansion cancelled by the mansion's owner. Despite her troubles with the show disrupting her job as a journalist, and her disagreements with how the show has an specific ideal of beauty, Kaufman still watches the episodes faithfully with an email group dubbed "Bach Discush" where they comment on what happens on each episode and who they think should win.

Bonus Downloads
*Get Free Books with **Any Purchase** of* Conversation Starters!

Every purchase comes with a FREE download!

Add spice to any conversation
Never run out of things to say
Spend time with those you love

Get it Now

or Click Here.

Scan Your Phone

Fireside Questions

"What would you do?"

Tip: These questions can be a fun exercise as it spurs creativity among the readers by allowing alternate scene endings and "if this was you" questions.

~~~

question 21

Kaufman is known for revealing hidden secrets in Hollywood as a journalist. Do you think this may make her someone to be wary of? Why or why not?

~~~

~~~

question 22

As a journalist, Kaufman has developed thick skin. Do you think that it bothered her to be called names such as "moron" by the creator of her favorite show?

~~~

~~~

question 23

When it comes to secrets such as sexual harassment, how do you think Kaufman was able to learn about the hidden secrets?

~~~

~~~

question 24

Kaufman has commented on her notice of how the show's contestants look the same when it comes to body type. How do you think she feels when she sees the same type of women on the show?

~~~

~~~

question 25

Kaufman has been to notable award shows such as The Academy Awards. How do you think she felt as she worked at these award shows?

~~~

~~~

question 26

If you were chosen to be a contestant on *The Bachelor*, how would you feel?

~~~

~~~

question 27

What would you do if you were chosen to be on the show? Would you accept? Why or why not?

~~~

~~~

question 28

The Bachelor is an extremely popular show in America. Do you think it would hold as much popularity in other countries? Why or why not?

~~~

~ ~ ~

question 29

What would you do if you were Amy Kaufman and had the opportunity to go behind the scenes of your favorite reality show. Which show would you choose to expose?

~ ~ ~

~~~

question 30

Do you think if Kaufman had written about a different reality show, her book would have had as much success?

~~~

Quiz Questions

"Ready to Announce the Winners?"

Tip: Create a leaderboard and track scores to see who gets the most correct answers. Winners required. Prizes optional.

~ ~ ~

quiz question 1

True or False: The producers kept track of the contestants periods.

~ ~ ~

~~~

quiz question 2

True or False: The producers allowed as many alcohol drinks as the contestants wanted with little reinforcement of the 'two drink per hour' rule.

~~~

~~~

quiz question 3

Producers create the falling-in-love feeling by putting the contestants in _____ situations.

~~~

~~~

quiz question 4

Contestants sign a _____ to let the
producers use any personal information.

~~~

~~~

quiz question 5

True or False: Contestants are allowed to use the internet and cell phones during the show.

~~~

~~~

quiz question 6

True or False: Contestants have all different kinds of body-types on the show.

~~~

quiz question 7

Producers were able to book events and transportation for _____ when creating the show.

~~~

quiz question 8

True or False: Amy Kaufman is an editor of the *LA Times.*

~~~

~ ~ ~

quiz question 9

True or False: Kaufman writes profiles of various stars.

~ ~ ~

~~~

quiz question 10

The first sexual harassment Kaufman revealed was
that concerning actor _____.

~~~

quiz question 11

True or False: Kaufman revealed the sexual harassment claims of Bill Cosby.

~ ~ ~

~~~

quiz question 12

Kaufman was _____ from ABC events after her book's publication.

~~~

Quiz Answers

1. True
2. True
3. High-stress
4. Contract
5. False
6. False
7. Free
8. False
9. True
10. James Franco
11. False
12. *Banned*

Ways to Continue Your Reading

EVERY month, our team runs through a wide selection of books to pick the best titles for readers and reading groups, and promotes these titles to our thousands of readers – sometimes with free downloads, sale dates, and additional brochures.

Click here to sign up for these benefits.

If you have not yet read the original work or would like to read it again, you can purchase the original book here.

Bonus Downloads
*Get Free Books with **Any Purchase** of Conversation Starters!*

Every purchase comes with a FREE download!

Add spice to any conversation
Never run out of things to say
Spend time with those you love

Scan Your Phone

On the Next Page...

If you found this book helpful to your discussions and rate it a 4 or 5, please write us a review on the next page.

Any length would be fine but we'd appreciate hearing you more! We'd be very encouraged.

Till next time,

BookHabits

"Loving Books is Actually a Habit"